PREFACE

"When a writer crosses the sea of contemplations, the only thing that matters is how much that person romps around his or her own tract with ardour when no one else is watching, when no one else is acknowledging…."

I am grateful to my parents, my brother, my friends and some

of my teachers who
kept welcoming
some serious debates
and heated
arguments. Every
opinion, every
discourse, every
mockery, every
appreciation, every
defeat and every
scrutiny has
contributed to this
book.

I will be questioning
a few acts and
thought processes

through this book. People who are highly opinionated, I suggest you avoid this piece of art. By the end of this book, most of you are likely to receive the answers to those questions which keep bothering you.

So, this is not some unusual contemplation (Could turn unusual for some though.)

I strongly believe

that some incidents,

some losses and

some actions come

together and make

every story-

extraordinary!

A part of me will never
surrender

A part of me will seldom
accept

A part of me will always
stay tender

A part of me will often
detest

The Upbringing

Parenting – is one of
the most admired
roles in our society
where inhibitions
play simultaneously.
Sans sanity, it's
sometimes like
going on a foray. I
know I am not too
old to delve in this
very strong
emotional
commotion, still I
find myself fit
enough to at least

cross question some of the vital characteristics of "The Upbringing".

When a child is born, power, I repeat, it is power that stems from the mother's womb. Father, at the same time, finds himself superior and better than those who roam around with lesser responsibilities.

These two figures
get so busy playing
their respective roles
that they almost
forget the child they
are raising is not a
toy. Child's choices,
behaviour,
reactions,
observations come
to the fore only after
the two are done
playing their
respective roles.

Let me be very clear
here, I am talking

about those families that I have observed around me. It's very well understood that there were, there are and there will always be exceptions.

No, I am not digressing from the subject. I am on it. As a kid, I always pranced around with questions like why girls load up their faces with

make-up? Why do
parents ignore when
their child does not
like something?
Why do they beat or
scold their child
sometimes, in front
of the known
people?

Why can't they bear
the sight of their
child losing a
competition or a
game? Why do they
run away from the
questions that are

logical? There were so many 'Why' but so less 'That's Why'.

Initially, I was not a great performer. I was more into enjoying little things (still I enjoy little things after all little creatures like squirrels instantly bring out the child in me.) around me like playing with my brother, cousins and friends. But, at the

same time, I used to
observe
personalities like
how they are
pretending, how
they are trying hard
to be all innocent,
when they are not,
how they are all
helpless in front of
their family
members, etc. etc. I
remember those
friendships wherein
I was asked to be all
good every time and
I clearly remember

those rivalries
wherein I was just
'me' with a feeling
of comfort and
contentment deep
down.

Of course, I always
had my
apprehensions but
that didn't deter me
from looking at or
identifying with
what I truly wanted.

Let's accept this –
we live in a world of
hypocrites. I am

sure most of you
can't even think of
saying your mind
out in front of those
you think you love.
You simply love the
idea of being
attached to
someone, and you're
shit scared of losing
those who form
your inner circle,
circle on which you
entirely rely.

As a child, I received
so many suggestions

from my relatives,
teachers, my
parents, even
acquaintances and I
value those still. But
those suggestions
did not deviate me
from questioning
what was
happening around
and it grieves me
when I think about
millions little lives
around who often
spend their entire
childhood receiving
a lambasting from

their parents or relatives for being blunt.

To be precise, I was weird. Whenever someone said – "You can't do this". I ended up doing that. It was class VI. I was told that I can't study Sanskrit. Why? Because in my previous school, the syllabus didn't keep space for Sanskrit and my

current school was
so damn sure that
this child (I)
wouldn't be able to
pick this subject.
Anyway, I studied
and started liking
this subject.
Consequently, I
cleared my
examination with a
good score which
was enough to
surprise my Sanskrit
teacher. Teachers,
most of them, have
their own set of

assumptions and
they somehow like
sticking to those.
You know why?
Their orientation
doesn't allow them
to look beyond some
studies or
theoretical
extravaganza and
it's not entirely their
fault. It's actually
the conditioning of
their 'mind' which
often asks them to
behave in a
particular pattern.

Some of them
choose to break the
pattern whereas,
some like clinging to
the irrelevant and
impractical pattern.

This is to all the
parents. Don't you
dare forget that the
teachers are after
all, human beings
like you and me and
for some of them,
teaching is a legit
business. They are
less concerned with

transforming lives
for good and more
concerned about
their own growth in
the field of
education. Once
they spot a student
scoring well, they
start working on
him or her, whereas,
kids who are
mentally weak or
find it difficult to
comprehend, keep
struggling
somewhere with

those little hopeful eyes.

So, when a teacher says something like "You must ask your daughter or son to join dance classes or you must ask him or her to give extra time to a particular subject", shoot questions. Ask them why? Ask your child in front of them, "Do you really want to do this"? If the child

says 'No',
acknowledge that.
Yes, acknowledge it
and later when
you're home, talk to
your child about
everything. My
parents used to do
this. They did take
suggestions from
everyone around
but they never
ignored what my
brother and I
actually wanted.

"Show off" is
another hell of a
ride for any child.
Why do parents like
to flaunt the
accolades of their
child? Why do they
often fail to work on
the overall
personality of their
child?

Why do they behave
like morons when
their child fails a
minor subject test?
Why do they ask

their child to exhibit
his or her skill set
amid some
acquaintances?
Why can't they take
"No" from their
child if he or she is
unwilling? Why
does the child think
twice or thrice
before sharing
something
disconcerting, with
parents? Why does a
place like home
often fail to
celebrate the

existence of a child? What's wrong with this whole parenting thing?

Clear answer to all these questions is – constant societal pressure which is nothing more than a notion. The truth is – We don't want failures and we yearn for convenience more than rationale. We prefer doing

anything and
everything to
succeed and all that
is enough to ruin
"Life".

PATRIARCHY & FEMINISM – A BLACK HOLE

After spending five very bright years in New Delhi – capital of India, North Campus, I was clueless for some time. I met guys who were very studious, ambitious and very serious about their career and life.

Some of them were pretending, and I

must say, they were really good at it, but a few were genuine too. They knew what they want and how to pursue. I won't get into the gender specific actions or thought process because that's irrelevant.

Let's dig deep. I had come across this very fascinating Sanskrit word – 'Ardhanareshvara'

which depicts a
half-male and a
half-female, equally
split down the
middle. It means 'the
Lord who is half
woman'. It clearly
shows that the male
and female
principles are
inseparable, which
further elucidates
the unity of
opposites in this
world and the
universe. "Totality
that lies beyond

duality" – is what
we all need to
ascertain.

Women across the
globe are more
powerful,
independent and
straight forward
now as compared to
the bygone era.
These qualities did
not come that easy
to us and we know
it very well.

Things that I am
going to put across

in the subsequent
lines may not add
much to your box of
'acceptable things'.
A lot of women are
not at peace, they're
becoming cynical
and they're facing a
lot of problems as
far as relationships
are concerned.

When the whole
world embraced the
idea of feminism
and when feminism
started laying its

foundation in books,
discussions and
actions worldwide,
the most basic
thought was to
make women
independent and
strong enough to
put across their
ideas and lead in
their own beautiful
ways.

However, only a
part of it recklessly
crossed the streets,
minds and

consequently
became an antidote
to women's hard
times at numerous
levels. So, will it be
insane if I say earlier
it was 'Patriarchy'
and now it is
'Feminism'?

When we talk about
feminism, it should
mean equal rights
and equal
opportunities for
women. But let me
tell you, a lot of

women do degrade
men at different
levels under the veil
of 'feminism'.
Patriarchy anyway
was taking a lot
from us, sadly, it is
feminism now.
Women need to
understand 'women'
first. I have been a
victim of hatred
emanating from the
ones (mostly
women) who
claimed they knew
me.

At workplace, I have noticed women being all jealous and less accommodating when it comes to accepting another woman who is better or brighter than them. Rather than learning from that woman, they tend to belittle her on different occasions, even worse; they tend to ignore her presence.

It's time I share a real incident with you all. There was a girl who was not on my company's payroll like I was. This shouldn't have been the matter of discomfort for her, still, this fact somewhere kept bothering her too much as she found me intimidating, I guess.

She never even tried
to hold a
conversation, never
tried to know what I
was going through. I
was new to the city,
and mind it, 'Guys'
Yes, 'guys' helped
me and made me
feel at home more
than any woman or
women around me.

She finally managed
to cross all the limits
one day, when we
bumped into each

other in the washroom. She had the audacity to say – 'Hey listen, I am sorry but I can't like you'. That was 'it'. I kept myself calm as I never wanted any drama, hence, replied – 'Are we getting paid to like or dislike someone here?' No right? So, it just doesn't matter if you don't like me. You better concentrate on your work.'

That day itself I had to inform my reporting manager about this episode. Sometimes, it becomes extremely important to voice up. I was facing her indirect taunts, her subtle wrath almost on a daily basis, because I was being hopeful.

I was trying to
understand her, I
was trying to make
her comfortable in
her own space but
you know what, if
someone is
reluctant, if
someone is already
full of opinions and
want to feed those
opinions regularly,
every step and every
effort swiftly meets
the dead end. Then
it's all about taking
some concrete

action against that person.

I would say I was blessed enough as my reporting manager after knowing this whole thing clearly asked me – 'Do you want me to take this up with the HR?' I refused. I said 'No'. I just want you to tell her that she should better focus on her goals and not me. I am there to help her though. Why did I bring this episode up?

All you women out there, better start supporting other women or just forget about standing against 'patriarchy'. It doesn't suit you. Stop being a hypocrite.

First of all, it's not just about

'patriarchy' or 'feminism'. It is more about understanding the differences and individualities that surround us. Patriarchy and Feminism both stem from the gender gap/s and all these years, since time immemorial I would say, we have been taking the gender part too seriously.

Yes, it is important
to acknowledge that
'he is a man', 'she is
a woman', but tell
me one thing, who is
going to
acknowledge that he
is an individual and
she is an individual?
Gods? Saints? Who?
Shouldn't we be the
ones acknowledging
it, considering it
every time? Shame
on us seriously.

QUESTIONING THE LABELS

Once we join the platoon of achievers, labels follow. Labels are like marijuana. When you taste it for the first time, you fly. You get high and stop noticing what's coming along. Similarly, labels compress our personalities in some ways.

Labels constantly
ask us to perform in
one particular
direction, in a
particular way, for a
particular period,
for a particular
section of society.
Something
disappointing here
is – 'We tend to lose
the uniqueness that
makes us who we
really are while
carrying the burden
of various labels.

Labels are not bad. Primarily, labels drive us every time we fall or lose focus. Still, every now and then, it's important to get rid of those labels and experience things as they are.

Let me share a trivial yet very disturbing example. You go out on a date and you start asking about his or her job profile including the annual salary and designation. It is important, no doubt, but I believe one can make money, however, a healthy relationship is as rare as spotting a snow leopard in Ladakh.

And, here are those bigger questions that arise amid all this – Do we keep ourselves open

enough to explore
the hidden? Do we
keep ignoring the
ubiquitous truths
from time to time
while we are on the
run for glory? How
much are we really
willing to change
things around us for
better?

A very important
part of our life goes
in imbibing. We
imbibe from home,
from school, from

universities, from
job and from
various other places.
And the result is
clear. We do have
winners, leaders and
people with
different
designations, except
people with some
courage, some
empathy, some
affection and some
rationale.

So, this was part one folks. For

more surprises, stay tuned.....!

Special Thanks to you my friend

-Kartik Maurya. You have

created a celestial book cover

and I love it...!

www.ingramcontent.com/pod-product-compliance
Lightning Source LLC
Chambersburg PA
CBHW051125250726
48655CB00007B/2894